Surprisingly Simple:

LLC vs. S-Corp vs. C-Corp
Explained in 100 Pages or Less

Surprisingly Simple:

LLC vs. S-Corp vs. C-Corp
Explained in 100 Pages or Less

Mike Piper

Dedication

For those who have the courage to dream,
That you may also have the courage
To go beyond just dreaming.

Table of Contents

Introduction   7
    Why entity selection is so crucial
    Is this book for you?

Part One
Sole Proprietorships & Partnerships:

1. Sole Proprietorships—Overview   12
    How to form one
    How to know if you need a D.B.A.

2. Sole Proprietorships—Taxation   17
    "Pass-through" entities
    Self-employment tax on profits

3. Sole Proprietorships—Legal   22
    Unlimited liability
    Is unlimited liability really that
      big of an issue?

4. Partnerships—Overview &
  How to Form Them   25
    Federal, state, and local requirements
    Why you need a partnership agreement

5. Partnerships—Taxation   30
    Pass-through entities
    Form 1065
    Schedule K and K-1
    Self-employment tax

6. Partnerships—Taxation (Part 2) Tax Basis   35
    What is tax basis?
    What increases or decreases tax basis?

7. Partnerships—Legal   39
    Unlimited liability-even for each other!
    Partners as agents of the partnership
    Limited partnerships

**Part Two
Your Other Options:
LLC, C-Corp, or S-Corp**

8. LLCs—Overview & How to Form Them   45
    Articles of Organization
    Qualifying in other states
    Why you need an operating agreement
    Transitioning from a sole proprietorship
    Transitioning from a partnership
    Do it yourself or get help from a pro?
    Who is allowed to form an LLC?

9. LLCs—Taxation   54
    What it means to be a disregarded entity
    Electing C-corp or S-corp taxation
    State taxation of LLCs

10. LLCs—Legal   60
    Generally offer limited liability
    When limited liability doesn't apply

11. C-Corporations—Overview &
    How to Form Them   63
    Do-it-yourself or get professional help?
    Tax consequences of forming a C-corp
    Who can't form a C-corp

12. C-Corporations—Taxation   67
    Pay income taxes on their own profits
    Double taxation of dividends
    Paying yourself a salary
    Potential for savings: Income splitting
    Corporate losses
    Qualified Personal Service Corporations

13. S and C Corporations—Legal   75
    Corporations are their own legal entities.
    Excellent limited liability
    Ongoing legal requirements
    "Piercing the corporate veil"

14. S-Corporations—Overview &
How to Form Them 80
Legally the same as C-corporations
Electing S-corp taxation: Form 2553
Who's eligible for S-corp taxation?

15. S-Corporations—Taxation 83
Pass-through taxation
No self-employment tax!
Determining a "reasonable salary"

Part Three
Two Final Considerations

16. Using Insurance to Limit Your Liability 88
What type of policy?

17. Other Related Costs 92
Accounting & tax preparation costs
Attorney's fees
Audit likelihood

Conclusion – Putting It All Together 98

Appendix: Helpful resource guide

Introduction

Much like the other books in the *"in 100 Pages or Less"* series, this book seeks to offer an easy-to-understand explanation of a rather technical topic. Nothing terribly special about that.

What sets these books apart from the crowd is the fact that they seek to offer that explanation in as concise a manner as possible. The assumption is that you want to determine what type of legal entity is best for your business, and that—after making that decision—you want to go back to running the business that you love (rather than reading another 300 pages about limited liability companies, S-corporations, and C-corporations).

Why the Question of Entity Selection is So Crucial

How you structure your business is going to affect a myriad of things from how much tax you'll have to pay on your profits, to how your business will be treated in a lawsuit, to what type of checking account your bank will let you open.

Make the right decision, and you'll be paying less tax; you'll know your personal assets are protected from lawsuits against your business; and you might even save yourself some money on accounting and legal fees.

Make the wrong decision, and you'll be throwing away money to Uncle Sam; you'll be wasting money on legal bills; and you'll be only a lawsuit away from losing your home and other personal assets.

The Goal of This Book

The primary purpose of this guide is to give you a basic understanding of the advantages and disadvantages of the various legal structures.

The goal is to give you enough information to make an educated decision for yourself as to whether your business should be a sole proprietorship, partnership, LLC, or corporation. The goal is *not* to make you an expert on any of the tax or legal matters discussed.

Quite in fact, after reading this book, it still might be a wise decision to meet with an accountant and/or an attorney to get some personalized advice.

So why bother reading the book at all? My hopes are as follows:

a) Some business owners will realize that the decision really isn't all that complicated, and that, for them, it's really a no-brainer. And...

b) Those of you who decide it would still be wise to visit with a professional will at least have a basic level of understanding ahead of time.

Having a ground-level understanding before meeting with a pro will both cut your meeting shorter (thereby saving you money) and give you some clue as to whose interests are really being served. After all—to steal an analogy from Warren Buffet—asking a lawyer if you need to incorporate is like asking a barber if you need a haircut.

A Brief Outline

This book is broken down into three main sections:

1) A discussion of the pros and cons of the default legal structures (sole proprietorships and partnerships), as it's most likely that your business is currently operating as one of the two.
2) An analysis of the advantages gained by forming an LLC, S-Corp, or C-Corp, as well as what you stand to lose by forming any of the above.
3) A brief overview of some other related topics, such as the option of using insurance to protect your personal assets instead of (or

in addition to) forming a corporation to gain that protection.

So let's jump right in and get started...

PART ONE

Sole Proprietorships and Partnerships: Good Enough, or Is It Time for a Change?

CHAPTER ONE

Sole Proprietorships: An Overview

According to the IRS, in 2007 (the most recent year for which such data has been published), 23 million Americans filed tax returns as sole proprietors. That's out of 142 million total returns filed for individuals.[1] This means that approximately 1 out of 6 American households are running businesses as sole proprietors. That's a lot of sole proprietorships!

So, why is it that there are more people running businesses taxed as sole proprietorships than there are people living in the state of New York?

For two reasons:

---

[1] See Statistics by Form available at:
http://www.irs.gov/taxstats/statsbyform/index.html

1) Sole proprietorships are very easy to form.
2) Many business owners don't actually stand to gain much by changing structures.

Doesn't Get Much Simpler Than This

All you have to do to form a sole proprietorship is start doing business. (At least, that's all the Federal government requires you to do.) That is, any business started by a single person is automatically a sole proprietorship unless the owner decides to take some action (such as incorporating) in order to become a different type of entity.

Local Requirements for Starting a Sole Proprietorship

It's likely that your state, county, or city might have somewhat more time-consuming (and money-consuming) requirements for forming a sole proprietorship than the Federal government does.

Depending upon what type of business you want to start, your city may require you to get a license of one sort or another, and that license may be accompanied by a license fee. (Luckily, the local fees for starting a business are usually fairly small.)

EXAMPLE: Matthew plans to start a business in Chicago. He's going to be working out of his home, buying antiques and selling them on eBay® for a profit. The City of Chicago requires Matthew to obtain a Home Occupation License for $250. Thankfully, he only has to renew the license every two years.

State and County Requirements: Will You Need a D.B.A.?

If you plan to do business under a name other than your own, your county or state will probably require you to file a "Doing Business As" (D.B.A.) statement. Sometimes, they may even require you to publish it in a local newspaper. (There are plenty of services that can handle this for you for a reasonable fee. See appendix for suggestions.)

The reason for requiring a D.B.A. is that states want to have a name on file for somebody who can be held accountable if a sole proprietorship breaks a law (or does something that would result in a civil lawsuit).

EXAMPLE: Let's say you have a new porch built by a local construction company named Decadent Decks. The porch ends up looking great, and everything appears to be fine. But then, just one week after the porch is built, it collapses while you're on it, and you break two ribs and a wrist from the fall.

You'll likely want to sue Decadent Decks for (at least) the cost of the medical bills. The only problem is that Decadent Decks is a sole proprietorship. (More on this later, but that basically means that it isn't a legal entity, and therefore cannot be sued.) And there is no way to tell from the name of the business who the owner is. Thankfully, your state required the owner of Decadent Decks to file a D.B.A., so they have his name on record. As a result, you'll be able to sue the owner directly.

Depending upon your state or county's rules, you may not be required to file a D.B.A. if you use your own name within the name of the business. However, other states will require you to get a D.B.A. if your business is named anything other than your exact legal name. For instance, some states would even require a D.B.A. for a Chris Dowdes to start a business called Chris Dowdes' Web Design.

Chapter 1 Simple Summary

- Sole proprietorships make up the bulk of businesses in the United States (by far).

- Sole proprietorships are so popular due largely to the fact that they are so easy to form.

- The Federal government doesn't require you to file any documents to form your sole proprietorship.

- Your city will likely require a business license to start a sole proprietorship, depending upon what type of business you plan to operate.

- Many states and counties require you to file a "Doing Business As" (D.B.A.) if you plan to use a name for your business that is not the same as your legal name.

CHAPTER TWO

Sole Proprietorships: Taxation

Much like forming a sole proprietorship, handling the taxes for a sole proprietorship is fairly simple. It really comes down to filling out just a few forms.

"Pass-Through" Taxation

Sole proprietorships are known as "pass-through" entities. What this means is that the profit (or loss) from the business is "passed through" to the owner of the business. Therefore, if you run a sole proprietorship, the profit from the business will show up on your regular individual tax return (i.e., Form 1040).

Schedule C

Schedule C[1] is the form that you'll use to compute the profit or loss from your business. As tax forms go, this one isn't terribly complicated. For the most part, it's just a list of all your revenues followed by a list of all your expenses.

The end-result of Schedule C is a figure known as your "Net Profit or Loss," which will be carried over to your Form 1040 and taxed at the regular individual income tax rates (as per the following charts).

Single (2010)

If taxable income is over:	But not over:	The tax is:
$0	$8,375	10% of the amount over $0
$8,375	$34,000	$837.50 plus 15% of the amount over $8,375
$34,000	$82,400	$4,681.25 plus 25% of the amount over $34,000
$82,400	$171,850	$16,781.25 plus 28% of the amount over $82,400
$171,850	$373,650	$41,827.50 plus 33% of the amount over $171,850
$373,650	no limit	$108,421.25 plus 35% of the amount over $373,650

---

[1] All Federal income tax forms are available for download at www.irs.gov/formspubs/index.html

Married Filing Jointly (2010)

If taxable income is over:	But not over:	The tax is:
$0	$16,750	10% of the amount over $0
$16,750	$68,000	$1,670 plus 15% of the amount over $16,750
$68,000	$137,300	$9,362.50 plus 25% of the amount over $68,000
$137,300	$209,250	$26,687.50 plus 28% of the amount over $137,300
$209,250	$373,650	$46,833.50 plus 33% of the amount over $209,250
$373,650	no limit	$101,085.50 plus 35% of the amount over $373,650

The Self-Employment Tax

In addition to being subject to regular income tax, earnings from a sole proprietorship are subject to the self-employment tax (SE Tax). The SE Tax is calculated (on Schedule SE) by multiplying your net earnings from self-employment by 15.3%.

At first glance, it may seem unfair to subject somebody to an extra tax simply because they are self-employed. However, the SE Tax is really just a substitute for the social security and Medicare taxes that are paid on salaries and wages for employees.

For employees, a social security tax of 6.2% and Medicare tax of 1.45% are withheld from each paycheck. Then the employer is required to pay a matching amount. As such, the employee is paying 7.65%, and the employer is paying 7.65% for a grand total of 15.3%. When you run a sole proprietorship, you are, in essence, both the employee and the employer, so you get stuck with both halves of the bill.

Deduction for One-Half of SE Tax

Because you're paying a little bit of extra tax (the 7.65% that your employer would be picking up if you were an employee), Congress decided it would be fair to allow you to claim a deduction for the extra tax paid. As a result, after using Schedule SE to calculate your self-employment tax, you get to enter—on line 27 of your Form 1040—an amount equal to one-half of your SE Tax as an "above the line" deduction.

Chapter 2 Simple Summary

- Sole proprietorships are known as "pass-through" entities because the income from the business is passed through to the owner, showing up eventually on his or her Form 1040.

- The profit or loss from a sole proprietorship is calculated on Schedule C.

- Earnings from a sole proprietorship are subject to the self-employment tax (in addition to being subject to the regular Federal income tax). The SE Tax is calculated as 15.3% of your net earnings from self-employment.

- Schedule SE is the form used to calculate the self-employment tax.

CHAPTER THREE

Sole Proprietorships: Legal

The primary downside to operating your business as a sole proprietorship requires little explanation. In essence, the problem is that a sole proprietor is personally liable for all of the debts of the business. This is known as having "unlimited liability."

To elaborate, if anybody successfully sues your business, they'll be able to come after your personal assets, not just the money that you have in your business checking account. To be perfectly clear, this means that—if the suit is for enough money—you could end up losing all of your personal savings, your car(s), your home, and anything else you have that might be of value. Everything.

Oh My Goodness That's Scary! (Right?)

For many people, just reading a description of what it means to have unlimited liability is enough to get them to start searching online for "how to form a corporation." And that's understandable.

But before you go and spend a substantial amount of time and money forming some other type of business entity, spend a little time thinking about how big of a problem unlimited liability really is for *your* business.

For instance, do you offer a service, or do you create and sell a product? In either case, imagine the worst-case scenario, and think about how bad it really is.

Let's say you provide a service. What's the worst thing that could happen if *everything* goes wrong with a client? Does the client lose millions and millions of dollars? Does the client need a trip to the hospital? Or, perhaps, is the worst-case scenario simply that the client is out the money that you charged them?

If you create and/or sell a product, do the same type of analysis. If everything goes as terribly wrong as you could possibly imagine, what happens?

If the worst thing that you can think of isn't really all that bad, then perhaps—despite nearly everything you read online—it isn't necessary to incorporate or form an LLC.

EXAMPLE: A self-employed author who writes and self-publishes science fiction novels probably doesn't have a great deal to worry about regarding liability issues. (I don't know about you, but I can't think of too many things that could go wrong for this business owner that would result in significant liability to anybody.)

Chapter 3 Simple Summary

- As a sole proprietor you will have "unlimited liability" for any debts of the business. This means that, in the case of a lawsuit, somebody could come after your personal assets as well as your business assets.

- Depending upon the nature of your business, it's at least *possible* that unlimited liability isn't that big of a problem.

CHAPTER FOUR

Partnerships: Overview & How to Form Them

As you'll soon see, partnerships are similar to sole proprietorships in many ways, beginning with the manner in which they're formed.

Federal Requirements

Just like a sole proprietorship is automatically formed when one person goes into business, a partnership is automatically formed when two or more people go into business. No official documentation is necessary for a partnership to be formed. As soon as a multiple-owner business begins operating, it's a partnership (unless the owners have already taken actions to incorporate or form an LLC).

While you don't have to file any documents to create a partnership, there is one thing that you'll need to do for the Federal government promptly after forming your partnership. You have to get an EIN (Employer Identification Number).

An EIN is to a partnership what a Social Security Number is to an individual. It provides the IRS with a way to keep track of your partnership.

The process of obtaining an EIN is fast and free. Just go to www.irs.gov and search for "EIN application." Answer some simple questions about your business, and within 5-10 minutes you'll have your new EIN.

Local Requirements

Of course, just like a sole proprietorship, a partnership will likely be required to file some documents at the city level.

Generally speaking, the local requirements (like the requirements for a sole proprietorship) tend to be based upon what type of business you are engaged in rather than what type of legal structure you use for your business. Most cities care more about whether you provide accounting services, lawn care services, or interior design services than they do about whether you're a sole proprietorship or a partnership.

There are two easy ways to find out what your local requirements are. If you're in a smaller municipality, go to your local city hall and ask. If you're in a larger city, a few searches online should get the job done.

State and County Requirements

Because partnerships almost always have a name separate from the names of the partners involved, they generally have to make some sort of "Doing Business As" or "Assumed Name" filing at the state or county level. Much like the case of forming a sole proprietorship, this filing is often accompanied by a filing fee. And, again, there are several services—one is mentioned in the appendix—that will (for a fee) help you with this filing if you'd rather not deal with it yourself.

Partnership Agreement

Though not required, it's strongly recommended that you draft some sort of partnership agreement soon after forming a partnership. A partnership agreement is simply a contract between the partners that outlines exactly how everything will be divided.

At the very least, a partnership agreement should cover:

- How expenses will be divided,
- How profits will be allocated,
- How profits will be distributed (as we'll see in Chapter 6, distributions of profit aren't always equal to allocations of profit),
- Which partners will be responsible for which tasks, and
- Under what circumstances a partner can sell his or her interest in the partnership to somebody else (if, for instance, one partner has decided she no longer wants to play a role in the business).

Chapter 4 Simple Summary

- If the owners don't take any action to incorporate or form an LLC, a multiple-owner business will be a partnership by default

- Partnerships are required to obtain an Employer Identification Number (EIN). The process is free and can be done easily at www.irs.gov.

- Most municipalities will require some sort of license to operate a partnership. Generally, the license required depends upon the type of services/products the partnership offers.

- Like a sole proprietorship, a partnership will generally be required to file something along the lines of a D.B.A. at the state or county level.

- It's not required, but a partnership agreement is certainly a good idea to prevent disputes from arising down the line.

CHAPTER FIVE

Partnerships: Taxation

To put it as concisely as possible, partnership taxation works very much like sole proprietorship taxation, but with an extra step in the middle in which the profit (or loss) gets allocated to the partners.

Partnerships themselves are not actually subject to Federal income tax. Instead, they—like sole proprietorships—are pass-through entities. While the partnership itself is not taxed on its income, each of the partners will be taxed upon her share of the income from the partnership.

Form 1065

Form 1065 is the form used to calculate a partnership's profit or loss. Filling out Form 1065 isn't much more difficult than filling out a Schedule C for a sole proprietorship. On the first page, you list the revenues for the business, list the expenses for the business, and then subtract the total expenses from the total revenues. It's exactly what you would expect.

On the second and third pages of Form 1065 you answer several yes/no questions about the nature of the partnership. For instance, you'll be asked whether any of the partners are not U.S. residents, whether the partnership had control of any financial accounts located outside of the U.S., and other questions of a similar nature.

Schedule K and Schedule K-1

The fourth page of Form 1065 is what's known as Schedule K. Schedule K is used to break down the partnership's income into different categories. For instance, ordinary business income goes on line 1, rental income goes on line 2, interest income shows up a little bit later on line 5, etc.

After filling out Schedule K, you'll fill out a separate Schedule K-1 for each partner. On each partner's Schedule K-1 is listed that partner's share of each of the different types of income.

EXAMPLE: Aaron and Jake own and operate a partnership. Their partnership agreement states that they're each entitled to exactly 50% of the partnership's income. If, on Schedule K, the partnership shows ordinary business income of $50,000 and interest income of $200, each partner's Schedule K-1 will reflect $25,000 of ordinary business income and $100 of interest income. This income will eventually show up on each partner's regular income tax return (Form 1040).

What's important to note here is that allocations from a partnership maintain their classification when they show up on the partners' individual tax returns. This is important because the tax rate on some types of income/gain is different than the rate on other types. For instance, long-term capital gains (gains from the sale of investments that were held for greater than one year) are taxed at a maximum tax rate of 15%.[1]

EXAMPLE: Aaron and Jake's partnership buys shares of a stock, holds the shares for several years, and then sells them for a gain of $10,000. When Aaron's $5,000 share of the gain shows up on his tax return, it still counts as a Long-Term Capital Gain (as opposed to counting as ordinary income). It will, therefore, be taxed at only 15%, even if Aaron is in a higher tax bracket.

---

[1] As of this writing, this rate is scheduled to increase to 20% at the beginning of 2011.

Self-Employment Tax for Partnerships

Ordinary business income from a partnership is generally subject to the self-employment tax when it is passed through to the partners. This makes sense given the rule that we just discussed about income maintaining its classification when allocated to a partner on his or her K-1.

Chapter 5 Simple Summary

- Like sole proprietorships, partnerships are "pass through" entities. A partnership is not subject to Federal income tax. Rather, its owners are subject to Federal income tax on their share of the profit.

- Form 1065 is used to calculate a partnership's profit or loss.

- Schedule K and Schedule K-1 are used to show each partner's allocated share of the profit/loss.

- Income (or gain) from a partnership maintains its original classification when it is passed through to a partner. As a result, long-term capital gains will be taxed at a maximum rate of 15%, and ordinary business income is subject to self-employment tax.

CHAPTER SIX

Partnership Taxation (Part 2: Tax Basis)

One thing that surprises the owners of many partnerships when their first tax season rolls around is the fact that partners get taxed on their allocated share of the partnership's profit, even if nothing was distributed to them. Don't worry—that may sound complicated, but it's really not that bad. The explanation has to do with a concept known as "tax basis."

The general rule is as follows: Owners of a partnership are taxed upon their share of the partnership's taxable income, regardless of how much is distributed. A partner is *not*, however, taxed upon distributions he receives from the partnership, so long as those distributions do not exceed the partner's tax basis in the partnership.

What does "tax basis" mean?

Tax basis refers to the amount of money a person has invested in an asset. A partner's basis in a partnership is:

1. Increased by any amounts he invests in the business.
2. Increased by his share of the partnership's taxable income (and decreased by his share of the partnership's losses).
3. Decreased by the amount of any distributions he receives.
4. Increased by his share of the debt owed by the partnership.

EXAMPLE: Michelle and Kayla run a partnership and have recently decided to bring on another partner to help with the work. Their friend Tim invests $20,000 and is given a 1/3 ownership interest in the partnership. At this point, Tim's tax basis in the partnership is $20,000.

During Tim's first year in the business, the partnership's taxable income is $90,000. Each partner will be taxed upon his or her share of the taxable income. Tim will be taxed upon $30,000 of income, and his tax basis in the partnership will be increased to $50,000. ($20,000 + $30,000)

In March of the following year, Tim receives a $35,000 cash distribution from the partnership. This is not taxable as income. The distribution does, however, decrease his tax basis in the partnership to $15,000. ($50,000 - $35,000)

In April, Tim receives another distribution, this time in the amount of $20,000. The first $15,000 of the distribution will be nontaxable and will reduce his tax basis to $0. The remaining $5,000 of the distribution, however, *will* be taxable, as his tax basis cannot be reduced below zero.

Tax Basis for LLC and S-Corp Owners

Like partnerships, S-corporations and multiple-owner LLCs are pass-through entities for Federal income tax purposes. (More on these topics in later chapters.) As a result, owners of those businesses—like owners of a partnership—are taxed upon their allocated share of taxable income and are not taxed upon distributions they receive (so long as those distributions do not exceed their tax basis in the business).

Chapter 6 Simple Summary

- In a partnership, the partners are taxed upon their allocated share of the taxable income, regardless of whether or not it is distributed.

- Partners are not taxed upon distributions received from the partnership, so long as those distributions would not reduce their tax basis below zero.

- A partner's tax basis in a partnership is increased by amounts he invests in the partnership, by his share of the partnership's taxable income, and by his share of the debt owed by the partnership.

- A partner's tax basis in a partnership is reduced by distributions received from the partnership and by his share of the partnership's losses.

CHAPTER SEVEN

Partnerships: Legal

It's obvious that before you form a partnership with somebody, you should make sure that he or she is a person you can trust and have confidence in. What's not necessarily as obvious is exactly *how much* you must trust this person before forming a partnership actually becomes a good idea.

Unlimited Liability—Even for Each Other!

Generally speaking, every partner in a partnership has unlimited liability for all of the partnership's debts. [Note: Limited Partnerships, which we'll be discussing momentarily, work somewhat differently.] It's very much like a sole proprietor's unlimited liability but with one crucial difference: You're now personally responsible for debts of the business, even if you had nothing to do with creating them.

EXAMPLE: Tom and Jennifer run a local newspaper, and their business is organized as a partnership. One week while Jennifer is on vacation, Tom reprints—without permission—an article from another newspaper. The other paper decides to sue for copyright infringement. Even though Jennifer had nothing to do with the legal infraction, the other newspaper can sue her for the entire amount of the debt, should it decide to. Such is the risk of being a partner in a partnership.

Of course, Jennifer could potentially be successful if she took Tom to court to sue for the amount that she ended up paying. But she'd still be out the cost of the legal fees, not to mention the hassle involved.

Partners as Agents of the Partnership

Each partner can be held responsible not only for liabilities resulting from a lawsuit, but also for liabilities stemming from a contract signed by only one of the partners. Such a situation is the result of the fact that each partner is what is referred to legally as an agent of the partnership. Each partner (agent) has the legal power to bind the partnership—and thus each of the partners—to a contract.

Fortunately, there are some limitations to a partner's power as an agent of the partnership. Most importantly, each partner can only act as an agent in affairs that are within the scope of the partnership's business. For example, if you run a retail store that sells locally grown produce, you don't have to worry about your partner buying a house under the name of the partnership. Given that the purchase of a house is clearly outside the scope of the business, your partner would have no power as an agent to bind the partnership to the contract.

Limited Partnerships

So far, our discussion of partnerships has been about what are known more precisely as "general partnerships." In addition to general partnerships, there is another form of partnership known as the "limited partnership." Generally speaking though, whenever somebody simply uses the term "partnership," he's referring to a general partnership.

Limited partnership taxation works the same way as general partnership taxation. The difference between the two structures is that, in a limited partnership, there are two types of partners: general partners and limited partners. General partners have unlimited liability for the debts of the partnership while limited partners do not. Limited partners (much like shareholders of a corporation) cannot lose an amount greater than their initial investment in the partnership. A limited partnership can have as many or as few of each type of partner as it wants, with the one notable exception that there must be at least one general partner.

One important rule about limited partnerships is that the limited partners cannot participate in managerial decisions or the day-to-day operation of the partnership. If they do, they'll lose their limited liability. Therefore, in many limited partnerships, the general partners are the original founders, and the limited partners are outside investors.

Chapter 7 Simple Summary

- In a general partnership (commonly referred to as simply a "partnership"), each partner has unlimited liability for all of the partnership's debts.

- Each partner, as an agent of the partnership, has the power to bind the partnership to a contract.

- Partners do *not*, however, have the power to bind the partnership to contracts that are clearly outside the scope of the business.

- In a limited partnership, limited partners have limited liability. They can only lose the amount that they initially invested. General partners in a limited partnership have unlimited liability.

- Limited partnerships can have as many or as few limited partners as they choose, but they must have at least one general partner.

- Limited partners cannot engage in the management or day-to-day operations of the partnership.

PART TWO

Your Other Options: LLC, C-Corp, or S-Corp

CHAPTER EIGHT

LLCs: Overview & How to Form Them

Having only been around since the late seventies, Limited Liability Companies (LLCs) are relatively new to the scene. (At least when compared to corporations, which have been around for as long as the United States.)

LLCs are created under state law, not Federal law, so the precise rules will vary somewhat from state to state. That said, the general idea behind the creation of the LLC was for it to provide business owners with the best of both worlds:

- The relative simplicity afforded by pass-through tax treatment (discussed in Chapter 9), and

- Limited liability protection (discussed in Chapter 10), previously only available through incorporation.

Forming an LLC: Articles of Organization

Again, the specifics vary from state to state, but in most states an LLC is formed by filing a document known as your Articles of Organization with the Secretary of State. Generally, your Articles of Organization must include:

- Your LLC's name and the address of its principal place of business,
- The names of the owners (referred to as the members) of the LLC,
- The nature of the LLC's business, and
- The name of the LLC's registered agent (the party authorized to accept delivery of legal documents—such as lawsuits—on behalf of the LLC).

Of course, your state may require your Articles of Organization to include other information in addition to the above.

Qualifying for Business in Other States

If you plan to do business in states other than the one in which your LLC is formed, you may be required to file some sort of documentation with the Secretary of State in each of those states. This process of filing with other states is known as "qualifying" or "foreign qualifying" your LLC in those states.

Generally, the question of whether or not you'll have to qualify your LLC in a state comes down to whether or not the LLC will have a physical presence in that state. A physical presence is just what it sounds like: An office, retail location, warehouse, etc. Having employees or a bank account in a state is also likely to make it necessary for your LLC to qualify there. The rules vary from state to state, so be sure to find out what the requirements are for the states with which your business will have any interaction.

Operating Agreement

If your LLC is going to have multiple owners, you should definitely create an operating agreement. An operating agreement does for an LLC what a partnership agreement does for a partnership. It outlines:

- How expenses will be divided,
- How profits will be allocated,
- How profits will be distributed (as with a partnership, distributions of profit aren't always equal to allocations of profit), and
- Which owners (members) will be responsible for which tasks.
- Under what circumstances a member will be allowed to sell his/her interest in the LLC.
- What occurs in the event of death or disability of one of the owners.

Transitioning from Sole Proprietorship to LLC

Generally, the move from sole proprietorship to limited liability company isn't terribly complicated. The primary reason for the ease of this transition is the fact that (as we'll see in the next chapter) the transition from sole proprietorship to LLC is a nontaxable event.

EXAMPLE: Kalinda runs a sole proprietorship working as a personal chef. She decides, for liability reasons, to form an LLC. After filing all the appropriate paperwork to establish the LLC, all she has to do is transfer the ownership of the business-related assets (business checking account, equipment, etc) to the LLC. This transfer of assets is referred to as a non-taxable event. That means that it will not have any impact on her Federal taxation for the year.

Transitioning from Partnership to LLC

The move from partnership to limited liability company isn't complicated either. The reason is (again) that the transfer of assets is a nontaxable event.

EXAMPLE: Eric and Karl are partners in an event planning business. Their business is growing, and they decide that it would be wise to form an LLC in order to limit their potential liability should something go wrong at one of their events. After forming the LLC, they transfer all of the assets that were previously owned by the partnership so that they are now owned by the LLC. This transfer impacts neither the Federal taxation of the business, nor the Federal taxation of either of the business's owners.

Do it Yourself, or Get Help from a Pro?

Should you decide to form an LLC, one of the questions you'll have to answer is whether you want to tackle the paperwork on your own or find a professional to take care of it for you. Generally your options break down into 4 different categories:

1. Find a local attorney,
2. Use an online service (such as mycorporation.com® or legalzoom.com®),
3. Buy a do-it-yourself kit (either software or a step-by-step guide), or
4. Do some research online and then form the LLC entirely on your own.

Of course, the obvious disadvantage of using an attorney is that it's going to be the most costly option. The tradeoff is that you're going to get somebody who knows your state's laws and who knows your personal situation.

Using an online service will generally cost less than hiring an attorney, and any reputable online service will know the filing requirements for all 50 states. The downside is that you won't get the personalized advice on which entity to choose. However—as discussed earlier—it's generally not that difficult of a decision for most business owners once they have access to all the relevant information.

Buying a do-it-yourself kit (whether a book that walks you through the process step-by-step or a piece of software that does the same thing) is going to cost even less than using an online service. If you find a guide with a good reputation—and you don't skip any steps—you're likely to do just fine with this alternative. However, be absolutely sure that the guide is written specifically for your state, otherwise it's quite possible that something important will be left out.

I generally recommend against attempting the process entirely on your own, regardless of how much research you've done online. Most people who take this approach seem to end up forgetting something important. Given the affordability of most of the services/do-it-yourself programs, it doesn't make sense not to get any help—especially when compared with the hassle of having to go back and change something later, or having to prepare some document in a rush because your banker or insurance agent needs to see it. There's even the possibility that, if you really mess up the formation process, your corporation won't even exist legally, and you'll think you're protected from personal liability when in reality you are not.

Who is Allowed to Form an LLC?

One final thing to note about forming an LLC is that, depending upon your business, you may not actually be eligible to form one. Many states have rules barring certain professionals, such as doctors, from forming an LLC. So, as always, be sure to check what your own state's rules are.

Sometimes, states that do not allow the above-mentioned professionals to form an LLC will allow them to form what is known as a Registered Limited Liability Partnership (RLLP). RLLPs are taxed the same way as regular partnerships—and thus, the same way as multiple-owner LLCs as we'll soon see.

The potential liabilities for partners in an RLLP are the same as for partners in a general partnership, but with one major exception: Partners cannot be held personally liable for lawsuits that arise as a result of another partner's malpractice. Each partner is, however, still liable for lawsuits arising from his or her own malpractice.

Chapter 8 Simple Summary

- The first document you'll have to prepare (in most states) when forming an LLC is your Articles of Organization.

- If you plan to have a physical presence, bank account, or employee in any state other than the one in which your LLC is formed, you'll likely be required to file some documentation with that state. This process is known as foreign qualification.

- If your LLC is going to have more than one owner, it's a very good idea to create an operating agreement to prevent disputes from arising in the future.

- Transferring assets from a sole proprietorship or a partnership to an LLC is not a taxable event (as long as the LLC is owned by the same people that owned the original business).

- It's generally not a wise idea to attempt the LLC formation process without getting any help.

CHAPTER NINE

LLCs: Taxation

Oddly enough, as far as Federal income taxes are concerned, LLCs don't really exist. The Internal Revenue Code—the body of law that outlines all Federal income taxation—treats each LLC as if it were one of the other types of entities (sole proprietorship or partnership usually).

Disregarded Entities

LLCs are referred to as "disregarded entities." They are referred to in such a manner because Federal tax law tends to disregard their existence.

EXAMPLE: Kali owns and operates a restaurant as a sole proprietorship. She later decides to form an LLC for her business. Because the LLC is a disregarded entity, the business will continue to be taxed as a sole proprietorship (for Federal tax purposes at least).

EXAMPLE: Steve and Beth own and operate a winery. After learning about the potential dangers of unlimited liability in a partnership, they decide to form an LLC. Because the LLC is a disregarded entity, the business will continue to be treated as a partnership for Federal income tax purposes.

In other words, single-member LLCs (LLCs with one owner) will generally be taxed as sole proprietorships, and multiple-member LLCs will generally be taxed as partnerships. Because of this tax treatment, LLCs—like sole proprietorships and partnerships—are often referred to as "pass-through" entities.

LLCs Taxed as Corporations

Sometimes, after forming an LLC, the owner(s) of the LLC will decide that they would benefit from being taxed as a C-corporation rather than as a sole proprietorship or partnership. (We'll cover C-corp taxation in Chapter 12.) When this happens, the owner(s) have two options:

1) Form a corporation and transfer all of the assets from the LLC to the corporation, or

2) Fill out a form (Form 8832)[1] electing corporate tax treatment.

The second option is certainly the easier and less costly of the two.

The same thing can be done should the LLC's owner(s) decide that S-corporation taxation would be beneficial. The only difference is that a different form (Form 2553) is used to notify the IRS of the election.

Is Electing Corporate Tax Treatment for Your LLC Really a Good Idea?

Filling out a form to elect corporate tax treatment is certainly easier than actually forming a corporation, transferring all the assets from your LLC to the corporation, and then dissolving your LLC. However, some tax professionals recommend rather strongly against electing corporate tax treatment for a Limited Liability Company.

The reason these tax advisors are hesitant to elect corporate taxation for an LLC is not that corporate taxation is a bad thing. Rather, they're concerned about the potential for problems resulting from two conflicting sets of laws. In other words,

---

[1] Again, all Federal income tax forms are available for download at www.irs.gov/formspubs/index.html.

they're uncomfortable with the situation resulting from a business being treated as an LLC for most legal purposes, but as a corporation for tax purposes.

State Taxation of LLCs

Again—unless an election is made otherwise—LLCs will be treated as either sole proprietorships or partnerships for Federal tax purposes. However, depending upon where your business is located, state income taxes might not work the same way.

In some states, LLCs are taxed, by default, in a manner roughly equivalent to the way that corporations are taxed. This makes for a rather complicated situation in which your business is treated as a sole proprietorship (or as a partnership if it has multiple owners) by the IRS, but as a corporation by your state.

Other states have a minimum annual income tax for LLCs (though it may be called something else). For instance, in California LLCs are subject to a "franchise tax," which is basically just an income tax, but with an annual minimum of $800.

EXAMPLE: Braden runs a sole proprietorship in California for his part-time video production business. He earns roughly $3,000 per year from the business and is considering forming an LLC. However, even with an annual income of only $3,000, a

California LLC would still be subject to a tax of $800, or over one-quarter of its total profit. Braden eventually decides that the benefits of forming an LLC would be outweighed by this disproportionately large tax.

Before deciding to form an LLC, it's definitely a good idea to find out precisely how your state taxes limited liability companies. Generally, you'll be able to find this information online without too much difficulty by searching for your state's Treasury Department, Department of Revenue, or corresponding organization.

Chapter 9 Simple Summary

- For Federal tax purposes, single-owner LLCs are treated as sole proprietorships, and multiple-owner LLCs are treated as partnerships.

- The owners of an LLC can elect to be taxed as a corporation by simply filling out a form. However, many tax professionals are leery about recommending that course of action as opposed to actually creating a corporation.

- Many states do not tax LLCs the same way that the Federal government does, so be sure to find out how your own state taxes LLCs before creating one.

CHAPTER TEN

LLCs: Legal

Generally speaking, the reason for forming an LLC is to obtain some protection from unlimited liability. And part of the reason that LLCs have become so popular in recent years is that they usually do a good job of providing such protection.

That said, the limited liability provided by an LLC is not perfect. So it's essential to determine whether or not the protection afforded by an LLC will be beneficial for your particular situation.

Rather than attempting to explain all the situations in which operating your business as an LLC *would* protect you, let's just cover the types of situations in which having an LLC would *not* protect you from personal liability.

Signing Personally for Business Debt

If the owner of an LLC personally signs for a loan for the business, the lender will be able to hold the LLC owner personally liable for payment of the debt, regardless of the fact that the business is an LLC.

Of course, the obvious lesson is to do everything possible to avoid personally signing for a business loan. Unfortunately, if your business is new, it's very likely that creditors will be unwilling to loan you a large amount of money unless you are willing to be on the hook for it personally.

Liability Resulting from Services Performed by the LLC Owner

Usually, if an owner of an LLC performs a professional service (e.g., accounting, health care, engineering, etc.) for a client, the client will be able to hold the owner personally liable for any damages caused by his malpractice.

Similarly, many states do not (yet, perhaps) have laws explicitly protecting LLC owners from the malpractice of other professionals in the firm (as compared to partners in an RLLP, for instance).

EXAMPLE: Karen, Christopher and Kyle are the owners of a dental practice, organized as an LLC. One day while performing oral surgery on a patient,

Kyle's attention wanders, and he ends up severely damaging a nerve, causing the patient to permanently lose feeling on one side of his face.

The client will be able to hold Kyle liable for the malpractice. In fact, it's at least possible that Karen or Christopher could be held liable as well.

Chapter 10 Simple Summary

- If you end up signing personally for a business loan, you're going to be held personally responsible for its repayment, regardless of the fact that your business is an LLC.

- LLC owners that perform professional services can still be held personally liable for their own malpractice.

CHAPTER ELEVEN

C-Corporations: Overview & How to Form Them

"Corporation: An ingenious device for obtaining profit without individual responsibility."

-Ambrose Bierce

Though the term "corporation" tends to conjure up images of large, modern companies, corporations have been around for centuries. In fact, forming a corporation (previously referred to as a "joint-stock company") was the original method for a business owner to receive protection from unlimited personal liability for his or her business.

The Two Types of Corporations

All corporations are either C-corporations or S-corporations. The only difference between a C-corp and an S-corp is the way in which each is taxed (we'll discuss this more fully in later chapters).

When a person uses the word "corporation," she may be referring to either C-corporations or to corporations in general (both C and S). You'll generally be able to figure it out from context without too much difficulty.

How to Form a Corporation

The options for forming a corporation are very much the same as for forming an LLC:

1) Attempt to research it and do it yourself,
2) Do it with the help of a how-to guide,
3) Use an online service, or
4) Enlist the aid of an attorney.

What makes the situation dramatically different from forming an LLC is the level of complexity. Forming a corporation requires a great deal more work, and there are many more things that could potentially be messed up. As such, I'd recommend rather strongly against attempting to do it on your own. I'd suggest using either an online service or a local attorney.

Tax Consequences of Forming a C-Corporation

As we'll discuss more fully in the next chapter, C-corporations are taxable entities. As a result, there will be tax consequences when you transfer the business-related assets into the name of the corporation.

Given that (unlike the formation of an LLC) the asset transfer will be a taxable event, it's probably a good idea to get a tax professional's advice on how to do the transfer. Depending upon your particular situation, it may be best to contribute (give) the assets to the corporation, to sell the assets to the corporation, or perhaps some combination of the two.

Who Isn't Eligible to Form a C-Corp?

In many states, there are a few particular professionals who aren't allowed to form a regular C-corporation. Instead, they're required to form a "qualified personal service corporation" (discussed in Chapter 12). Professionals who are frequently barred from forming a regular C-corp include:

- Accountants
- Doctors and other healthcare professionals (nurses, pharmacists, psychologists, etc)
- Engineers
- Lawyers
- Social Workers

This is one of those things that varies from state to state, so it's worth checking with your state's Secretary of State.

Chapter 11 Simple Summary

- Corporations can be either C-corporations or S-corporations. The only difference between the two is taxation.

- Forming a corporation involves much greater complexity than forming an LLC, so it's probably a good idea to enlist the help of an attorney as well as a tax professional.

- In many states, certain professionals are barred from forming a regular C-corporation. Instead they are required to form something known as a "qualified personal service corporation." (Discussed in chapter 12.)

CHAPTER TWELVE

C-Corporations: Taxation

Corporate taxation is unique in that the business itself is subject to an income tax. Note how this is different from a sole proprietorship or a partnership in which the business itself is not taxed, but the owners are taxed based upon their allocated share of the income.

A C-corporation's income tax is unaffected by how many owners (shareholders) the corporation has or by how much of the profit is distributed to the owners. C-Corporation income is taxed according to the following table:

Tax Rates for Corporations (2010)	
$0-$50,000	15%
$50,001-$75,000	25%
$75,001-$100,000	34%
$100,001-$335,000	39%
$335,001-$10,000,000	34%
$10,000,001-$15,000,000	35%
$15,000,001-$18,333,333	38%
Over $18,333,333	35%

Double Taxation of Dividends

When a corporation makes a distribution of earnings to its owners, the payment is known as a dividend. Dividend income is taxable to the recipient (though at a maximum rate of 15% as compared to ordinary income, which is taxed at the rates on pages 18 & 19).

In other words, corporate profits—if they are paid out to shareholders—are taxed twice: Once at the corporate level and once at the shareholder level.

Paying Yourself a Salary

One way to avoid the double taxation of the corporate structure is to pay the owners a salary—or year-end bonus—that will leave the corporation with exactly zero income. (Salaries paid to employees count as deductions for a corporation, thus reducing the corp's taxable income.)

Of course, the amount received as salary will still be taxable income to the owners. In fact, when a corporation pays its owners a total amount of salary equal to what profits would have been without the salary, the net result is actually exactly the same as if the business was simply being taxed as a sole proprietorship or partnership.

EXAMPLE: Debbie is the only owner of her business (a dietetics-consulting practice). Her business is currently a sole proprietorship, but she's attempting to determine if forming a C-corp would be beneficial. Her revenues for the year are projected to be $90,000, and her expenses (not counting any salary she pays herself if she incorporates) are projected to be $20,000.

If Debbie continues to run her business as a sole proprietorship, she'll have $70,000 of earnings from self-employment. (And regular income tax and self-employment tax will be computed as normal.)

If Debbie decides to incorporate and pay herself a $70,000 salary, the corporation will have a taxable income of $0. She'll have $70,000 of salary, upon which she'll pay regular income taxes. She won't have to pay self-employment tax. But she and the corporation will each be responsible for 7.65% of social security and Medicare taxes, totaling 15.3% anyway.

End result: Debbie pays the same total amount of tax in each scenario.

Potential for Savings: Income Splitting

But what if a business owner doesn't need every last dollar of her business's profits in order to pay her personal bills? Such situations are the reason why people sometimes discuss incorporation as a method to save on taxes.

Often, business owners can pay less total tax if they're comfortable leaving some money in the business's bank account. They can pay themselves a salary, but not a salary so large that it wipes out the corporation's profits entirely. The end result is that the corporation has some taxable income, and the owner has some taxable income. The tax savings are achieved because the income is split between the owner and the corporation (thus keeping them each in a lower tax bracket).

EXAMPLE: Let's use the same information from the example above and assume that Debbie has decided to incorporate. But we now have one more piece of information: Debbie lives a very simple lifestyle, and knows that she won't need all of the profits from the business in order to pay her personal bills. In fact, she only expects to need $30,000 of income in order to maintain her standard of living.

Debbie realizes that she can save money by splitting her taxable income. She decides to pay herself a salary of $30,000, and let the rest of the profits ($40,000) remain in the corporation's checking account. This way, the corporation has a taxable income of $40,000, and she has a taxable income of $30,000, and she ends up paying less total tax than she would if all $70,000 of income were taxable either to herself or to the corporation (as per the tax brackets on pages 18, 19, or 68).

Corporate Losses

Just like a corporation's taxable income is not passed through to the shareholders, a corporate loss is not passed through to the shareholders either. In other words, when a C-corporation incurs a loss for the year, that loss cannot be used to offset the owner(s) other taxable income.

Instead, when a C-corporation incurs a loss, it can use that loss to offset taxable income from the two prior years—if, in fact, there was any taxable income—or up to twenty years in the future.

In contrast, operating losses from pass-through entities *can* (with some limitations) be used by the owner(s) to offset their other taxable income.

Therefore, if you expect to incur losses during the initial years of your business, it may well be to your advantage *not* to form a corporation right at the outset.

EXAMPLE: Maria opens a specialty bakery in her neighborhood. Unfortunately, her business has a slow start, and she incurs a net loss of $15,000 in her first year of operation.

If her business is taxed as a sole proprietorship, Maria will likely be able to use the loss to offset some of the taxable income from her husband's job. If, however, her business is taxed as a C-corporation, Maria will not gain any immediate tax benefit from the loss. Instead, she will have to wait and use the loss to offset the corporation's income in future years.

Qualified Personal Service Corporations

As mentioned in the previous chapter, many types of professionals (doctors, lawyers, etc.) are barred from forming corporations in certain states. However, some states do allow them to incorporate.

The IRS is likely to treat such corporations as "Qualified Personal Service Corporations." This designation isn't a positive one. What it means is that the corporation's income will be taxed at a flat rate of 35%, rather than the rates shown on page 68, which begin as low as 15%.

Two requirements must be met for the IRS to assign the designation of Qualified Personal Service Corporation:

1. Substantially all of the corporation's activities are services performed in the fields of law, medicine, engineering, accounting, architecture, performing arts, actuarial science, or consulting.
2. 95% or more of the corporation's stock is owned by employees performing the above-mentioned services, or by retired employees, the estates of employees, or other people who acquired the stock as a result of an employee's death.

Chapter 12 Simple Summary

- Unlike sole proprietorships or partnerships, C-corporations are taxable entities. That is, they have to pay tax on the income they earn.

- After a corporation is taxed on its income, it can distribute it to the owners (in a payment known as a dividend). The owners are then taxed on the dividend income, thus resulting in two levels of taxation.

- It's possible to achieve some tax savings by utilizing income splitting if you think your business is likely to generate more income than you need for personal use.

- When a C-corporation incurs a loss, it cannot be used to offset the owners' other taxable income. The corporation can, however, use the loss to offset its income from the 2 prior years, or up to 20 years in the future.

- If a corporation is ruled to be a Qualified Personal Service Corporation, its income will be taxed at a flat rate of 35%.

CHAPTER THIRTEEN

Corporations: Legal

The essential thing to know about corporations is that, for legal purposes, they are distinct entities. In other words, corporations are treated (more or less) as if they were people. They're allowed to own things, rent things, sue or be sued, and so on.

Limited Liability

The reasoning behind the concept of the corporation—a business legally distinct from its owners—was to allow the owners to not have to worry about being held personally liable for the debts of the business. Generally speaking, because the corporation is a separate entity, anybody wishing to bring a lawsuit against the business has to bring it against the corporation rather than against the owners personally.

This protection is in fact one of the fundamental elements of our entire economy. As an example, what are the odds that anybody would have invested in PepsiCo® if they knew that they could be held personally liable if anybody were to bring a lawsuit against the company as a result of getting sick from one of their products? If corporations didn't offer the protection they do, hardly anybody would invest in new companies.

Planning on Outside Investment? Plan on Incorporating.

For the above-mentioned reason, if you're planning on securing cash from outside investors, it's quite likely that your only option is going to be to form a corporation. (To be more specific, it'll likely have to be a C-corporation due to S-Corporation ownership restrictions, which we'll discuss in Chapter 14.)

Another reason that investors are far more likely to invest in a corporation is that shares in a corporation can be sold far more easily than can ownership interests in any other structure of business. Investors like knowing that if they want to get out, they can.

Ongoing Legal Requirements

One slight drawback to forming a corporation is that there are a few ongoing legal requirements that will take up your time. For example, whenever the directors of a corporation make a major decision, most states require it to be recorded in a document known as a "resolution." A resolution doesn't have to be anything fancy or complicated. Just be aware that forming a corporation means you're going to be in for a little more paperwork.

Also, most states require an annual meeting of the directors and shareholders of the corporation, as well as a record of what was discussed at the meeting. Of course, if you're the only owner, this just means preparing one more document every year, as the "meeting" with yourself probably doesn't have to be very long.

"Piercing the Corporate Veil"

Whenever you read anything about the limited liability provided by the corporate form, you're also going to hear at least a mention of the term "piercing the corporate veil." This term refers to the fact that, on occasion, a court may decide that a corporation is not materially separate from its owners, and that the plaintiff should be allowed to come after the owners for their personal assets.

Some of the things that may lead a court to pierce the corporate veil include:

1. Intermingling of funds between corporate accounts and personal accounts of the owners,
2. Disregard for corporate formalities (such as the preparation of resolutions and holding of annual shareholder meetings),
3. Absence of corporate financial records, and
4. Anything else that would lead a court to believe that the corporation is merely a formality, and is not materially distinct from its owners.

Generally, the best thing you can do to prevent such an occurrence is to keep excellent records for the corporation. The most important records to make sure to keep are those detailing any transactions between the corporation and its owners.

Chapter 13 Simple Summary

- Generally speaking, the owners of a corporation will not be able to be held personally liable in the case of a lawsuit against the corporation.

- If you plan on attracting outside investors, you'll likely have to form a C-corporation.

- Major decisions made by the directors of a corporation must be documented in a corporate resolution.

- The directors and owners of a corporation are required to have a documented meeting every year.

- If a court decides that a corporation is not in fact distinct from its owners, the court may decide to "pierce the corporate veil," thereby allowing a plaintiff to come after the involved shareholders' personal assets.

- The best thing you can do to prevent a court from piercing the corporate veil is keep excellent records, especially for transactions between the corporation and its owner(s).

CHAPTER FOURTEEN

S-Corporations: Overview & How to Form Them

S-corporations are simply C-corporations that have elected (under Subchapter S of Chapter 1 of the Internal Revenue Code) to receive a special kind of tax treatment. In other words, the only difference between an S-corporation and a C-corporation is taxation.

Electing S-Corp Taxation

Electing S-corp taxation couldn't be any easier. All you have to do is fill out a single form (Form 2553), and your corporation will continue to be taxed as an S-corp for as long as you continue to meet the various shareholder requirements for S-Corp taxation (discussed next).

Also, as mentioned briefly earlier, LLCs are allowed to elect S-corp taxation by filing Form 2553.

Who Can Elect S-Corp Taxation?

In order for a corporation to be eligible for S-corp taxation, it must meet all of the following requirements:

1. It must be a domestic corporation (as opposed to a foreign one).
2. It must have no more than 100 shareholders.
3. The shareholders can only be individuals, estates, and tax-exempt organizations. (In other words, no corporations or partnerships as shareholders.)
4. It can have no nonresident alien shareholders.
5. It can have only one class of stock.
6. It cannot be a bank or insurance company.
7. All shareholders must consent to the election.

Chapter 14 Simple Summary

- The only difference between an S-corp and a C-corp is the way in which they are taxed.

- To elect S-corp taxation for a corporation or an LLC, simply fill out IRS Form 2553.

- In order to be eligible for S-corp taxation, a corporation must meet several requirements. (See list on previous page.)

S-Corporations: Taxation

S-corporations, like sole proprietorships and partnerships, are pass-through entities. That is, there is no Federal income tax levied at the corporate level. Instead, an S-corporation's profit is allocated to its shareholder(s) and taxed at the shareholder level.

Tax Forms for S-Corporations

An S-corporation's annual tax return is filed on Form 1120S. (This makes sense, given that a regular corporation's return is filed on Form 1120.) Form 1120S consists mostly of what you'd expect: A section detailing revenues, a section detailing expenses, and a section for allocating the corporation's taxable income among the shareholders. As with a partnership, Schedules K and K-1 are used to show how the business's profit or loss is allocated among the owners.

No Self-Employment Tax!

The big benefit of S-corp taxation is that S-corporation shareholders do not have to pay self-employment tax on their share of the business's profits.

The big catch is that, before any profits can be distributed, each of the owners who also work as employees must be paid a "reasonable salary." This salary will of course be subject to social security and Medicare taxes to be paid half by the employee and half by the corporation. As a result, the savings from paying no SE Tax on the profits only kicks in once the S-corp is earning enough that there are still profits to be paid out after paying the mandatory "reasonable salary."

EXAMPLE: Larissa is the sole owner of her S-corporation, an advertising agency. Her revenues from the business are $50,000 per year, and her annual expenses (not counting salary) total $10,000. Therefore, her S-corp's profit for the year (before subtracting her own salary) is $40,000.

Larissa's plan is to pay herself $30,000 in salary, and count the remaining $10,000 as profit, thus saving money as a result of not having to pay self-employment tax on the $10,000 profit.

Unfortunately, Larissa learns that the average advertising professional earns in the $60,000 range annually. As such, she's going to have a difficult time making the case that $30,000 is a "reasonable salary."

In the end, Larissa ends up setting her salary at $40,000 in order to avoid trouble with the IRS. Sadly, her S-corp's profit (after paying her salary) ends up being $0, so she isn't really saving any money on taxes as a result of S-corp taxation.

Determining a "Reasonable Salary"

So what's a reasonable salary? Good question. This exact question is frequently the topic of great debate in court cases between the IRS and business owners who are, allegedly, paying themselves an unreasonably small salary in order to save on self-employment taxes.

One way to get an estimate for reasonable salary is to visit salary.com®. There you can run a search, and it will tell you the average salary earned by people in your profession and in your geographical area.

Chapter 15 Simple Summary

- S-corporations are pass-through entities. That is, the corporation itself is not subject to Federal income tax. Instead, the shareholders are taxed upon their allocated share of the income.

- Form 1120S is the form used for an S-corp's annual tax return.

- Shareholders do not have to pay self-employment tax on their share of an S-corp's profits. However, before profits are calculated, any owners that work as employees for the S-corp will need to receive a "reasonable salary."

PART THREE

Two Final Considerations

Using Insurance to Limit Your Liability

One excellent piece of advice that many small business consultants give their clients is to consider using an insurance policy as a means of further protecting oneself from liability. Depending upon the situation, it may even be cost effective to use insurance *instead* of incorporating or forming an LLC.

What Kind of Policy?

Of course, when attempting to determine whether or not you'd want to get an insurance policy for your business, the first thing you need to figure out is what type of policy to shop around for. Generally, the best way to do this is to attempt to think of all the things that could go sufficiently wrong that they might result in a lawsuit.

When it comes to protecting yourself from liability to other parties, there are three primary types of insurance policies you should consider for your business:

1. General liability insurance,
2. Product liability insurance, and
3. Professional liability insurance (often referred to as "errors & omissions insurance" or "malpractice insurance.")

General liability insurance covers things such as a person coming into your retail location and slipping and falling on a just-washed floor. Product liability insurance covers precisely what it sounds like: liabilities caused by the product(s) you create and/or sell. Professional liability insurance covers you in case you make a mistake or neglect to do something important while providing services to a client.

Compare to Costs of Forming LLC/Incorporating/Etc

Perhaps, after reading this book, you'll have decided that you don't stand to gain anything from a tax standpoint by forming an S-corp or a C-corp. But you do think that you need a way to limit your liability. If that's the case, your options to limit your potential liability are to form an LLC, get an insurance policy, or both.

If you don't think it's necessary to form an LLC *and* get an insurance policy, a reasonable way to choose between the two would be to simply compare the cost of doing each of them. Be sure, in your comparison, to include ongoing costs of having an LLC, not just the cost of forming one. For instance, if your state imposes an extra income tax on LLCs, be sure to take that into account.

Chapter 16 Simple Summary

- Many times, it may be wise to get an insurance policy in order to help limit your potential liabilities from your business.

- The three main types of insurance policies for limiting liability from a business are general liability insurance, product liability insurance, and professional liability insurance.

- If you are trying to compare the costs of getting an insurance policy vs. forming an LLC, be sure to take into account the potential ongoing costs of having an LLC.

CHAPTER SEVENTEEN

Other Related Costs: Professional Costs & Audit Likelihood

As mentioned briefly in the previous chapter, there are likely to be ongoing costs associated with the type of business structure that you choose. In addition to the differences in taxation, the other big things to consider are accounting costs, tax preparation costs, attorney costs, and (maybe) audit costs.

Accounting Costs

For the most part, the accounting for an LLC is no more complicated—or expensive—than that for a sole proprietorship (or a partnership if the business has multiple owners). That said, the accounting for a corporation is significantly more complicated than accounting for a sole proprietorship or partnership. And, generally speaking, you can take "more complicated" to mean "more expensive," assuming you're going to be getting professional help.

The reason that corporate accounting is significantly more complicated is that corporations generally use a system known as double-entry bookkeeping, which is more complicated than the single-entry system used by most individuals and sole proprietorships. Generally, most small businesses that use double-entry bookkeeping will outsource it to an accounting professional, but some choose to do it on their own with the assistance of specialized software. (The most popular software being Intuit's QuickBooks®.)

Tax Preparation Costs

Like they do with bookkeeping, many small business owners choose to outsource their annual tax preparation. Tax preparation costs vary significantly depending upon your geographical location and the level of expertise of the tax professional.

Likely, the single biggest thing that affects the cost of tax preparation is the type of business entity that you've chosen. Tax prep for a sole proprietorship is the easiest (and thus cheapest), followed by

LLC tax prep, then partnerships, then C-corporations, and finally S-corporations.

A 2009 survey done by the National Society of Accountants can provide us with a little bit of hard data. According to the survey,[1] the average rates for tax preparation in 2009 were as follows:

Sole Proprietorship	$212
Partnership	$551
S-Corporation	$665
C-Corporation	692

The average rates include only Federal returns. Also, while they don't separately state the average rate for tax preparation for an LLC, we can probably safely assume that the cost would be just slightly above that for a sole proprietorship (if it's a single-member LLC) or that for a partnership (if it's a multiple-member LLC).

Attorney's Fees

One more thing to be sure to include in your decision as to which structure to choose is the ongoing attorney costs that are probable to arise as a result of having a more complicated legal structure. While it's impossible to quantify ahead of time, you can

---

[1] Available at http://www.nsacct.org/about_nsa.asp?id=642

certainly assume that operating a corporation will involve more attorney fees than either an LLC or a sole proprietorship.

Audit Likelihood

A question many business owners frequently ask is what impact—if any—a particular action will have upon their likelihood of being audited. Which legal structure you choose will significantly affect your chance of being audited.

According to the IRS Data Book[1], the chances of being audited in 2006 were as stated in the following table. Naturally, the IRS doesn't give separate data for LLCs. Again, as far as the IRS is concerned, a single-member LLC is the same thing as a sole proprietorship, and a multiple-member LLC is the same thing as a partnership.

Sole Proprietorships:	
Gross receipts under $25,000	1.30%
Gross receipts $25,000-$100,000	2.04%
Gross receipts over $100,000	4.31%
Partnerships:	0.42%
S-corporations:	0.45%
C-corporations:	1.33%

---

[1] Available at
www.irs.gov/taxstats/article/0,,id=168593,00.html

There are two main lessons from this data:

1. If you're a sole proprietor, your chance of being audited decreases significantly as a result of incorporating.
2. Regardless of which business structure you use, your chance of being audited in any given year is quite low.

Chapter 17 Simple Summary

- Accounting costs for a corporation are likely to be higher than those for a sole proprietorship or LLC.

- Tax prep fees for an LLC are likely to be slightly higher than those for a sole proprietorship (due to the potential for extra forms that need to be filled out for your state). And tax prep fees for a corporation are likely to be higher than those for an LLC.

- Generally, you're likely to incur more attorney fees when running a corporation than you will when running a sole proprietorship or a partnership.

- Your likelihood of being audited is far higher as a sole proprietorship than it is for any other business structure. That said, your chance of being audited is quite low either way.

CONCLUSION

Putting It All Together

There are two primary reasons that a business owner might want to change from being a sole proprietorship or partnership to a different form of business:

1. To save on taxes, and
2. To limit potential liability from the business.

Saving on Taxes

Forming an LLC isn't going to save a person any money on taxes. In fact, the IRS doesn't even recognize LLCs as a legal structure. Instead, it "disregards" them, treating single-member LLCs as sole proprietorships and multiple-member LLCs as partnerships.

Forming a C-corp has the potential to save a business owner money on taxes, but only if he expects to earn more from the business than he'll need for personal use. That is, if you plan to withdraw all of the earnings from your business, forming a C-corp is only going to cost you money. However, if you plan to leave some of the profits in the business, and eventually use them for business expansion, it's possible that forming a C-corp will save you money as a result of splitting the income between yourself and the corporation.

The big benefit of S-corporations is that distributions of S-corp profits are not subject to the self-employment tax. That said, before you can achieve any savings as a result of tax-advantaged profit distributions, you'll have to pay all the employee-shareholders a "reasonable salary." This salary will be subject to social security and Medicare taxes, which will total the same percentage as the self-employment tax anyway. You will, therefore, only save any money if your profits are large enough that there will be some remaining after paying the required "reasonable salaries."

Limiting Potential Liabilities

When it comes to limiting a business owner's potential liabilities from the business, just about anything is better than a sole proprietorship (or better than a partnership if it's a business with multiple owners).

LLCs go a long way toward limiting the liabilities of the owner(s), but the protection they offer is still not perfect. For example, having an LLC will not protect business owners from liabilities that result from their own professional malpractice. Nor will having an LLC protect a business owner from being held liable for a business loan for which she personally signed.

Corporations (both S-corps and C-corps) provide a similar degree of liability protection to that provided by an LLC. In some cases, a court may decide that a corporation is not, in essence, an entity distinct from its owners and that, as such, a plaintiff should be allowed to come after the corporation's shareholders for their personal assets. Such a decision is referred to as "piercing the corporate veil." The best thing a corporation's owners can do to prevent a court from making such a decision is to keep excellent records of every transaction, especially transactions between the corporation and its owners.

In some cases, the best method for a business owner to protect herself from liabilities from the business doesn't even involve changing the business's legal structure. Rather, it's to get an insurance policy to protect against such potential debts.

Two Final Thoughts

If you're still not certain which entity is the best for you, it's probably a good idea to discuss the issue with an attorney and/or tax professional.

Also, remember that, for many business owners, a perfectly reasonable option is to remain a sole proprietorship (or partnership) for the time being and to resolve to revisit the decision in another year or so.

APPENDIX

Helpful Resources

Note: While the resources listed below are generally regarded as being of high quality, their mention here does not imply an endorsement by the author or publisher.

www.irs.gov
> The IRS's website. *Remarkably* good for a governmental organization.

www.simplesubjects.com/tax
> The publisher's website. Includes a wide variety of tax information for small business owners.

www.taxalmanac.org
> An excellent compendium of tax research resources, including a wonderful discussion board.

www.legalzoom.com
> This site can help you with filing a DBA for a sole proprietorship, help with forming an LLC, or help should you decide upon incorporating.

www.quickbooks.com and www.quicken.com
> Run by Intuit®, these two programs are excellent bookkeeping resources. QuickBooks® is generally what I'd recommend, but if you want a more simplified version, go with Quicken®.

www.nolo.com
> The most well known (and deservedly so) publisher of legal self-help books. Useful for everybody; essential for business owners.

IRS Publications

Publication 334 – Tax guide for small businesses.

Publication 535 – Business expenses.

Publication 463 – Travel, entertainment, gift, and car expenses.

Publication 587 – Business use of your home.

Publication 946 – How to depreciate property.

Publication 541 – Partnership Taxation

Publication 542 – Corporate Taxation

Publication 505 – Tax withholding and estimated tax.

Also by Mike Piper:
Surprisingly Simple: Independent Contractor, Sole Proprietor, and LLC Taxes Explained in 100 Pages or Less

Find all of the following topics:

Business Taxation 101: A brief primer on tax topics in general, especially as they apply to businesses.

Home Office Deduction: How to ensure you qualify for it and how to calculate it.

Estimated Tax Payments: When and how to pay them, as well as an easy way to calculate each payment.

Self-Employment Tax: What it is, why it exists, and how to calculate it.

Business Retirement Plans: How to decide which type is best for your business.

Numerous Business Deductions: Several deductions explained in detail.

Audit Protection: What records to keep in order to protect yourself in case of an audit.

INDEX

A

Articles of Organization ·
46, 53
Audits · 92, 95

C

Capital Gains · 32, 34
C-Corporations · 7, 9, 44,
55, 63-67, 69, 71-72, 74,
76, 79-80, 82, 90, 94, 96,
98, 100

D

D.B.A. · 14-16, 27, 29
Deductions · 20, 69
Disregarded Entities · 54-
55
Dividends · 68, 74

F

Form 1040 · 17-18, 20-21,
32
Form 1065 · 30-31, 34

Form 1120 · 83, 86
Form 2553 · 56, 80-82
Form 8832 · 56

G

General Partnerships · 41-
43, 52

I

Incorporating · 9, 13, 23,
25, 29, 46, 69-70, 72, 76,
88, 90, 96
Insurance · 9, 51, 81, 88-
91, 100
Internal Revenue Code ·
54, 80
Internal Revenue Service ·
12, 26, 56-57, 72-73, 82,
85, 95, 98

L

Limited Liability
Companies · 7-9, 23, 25,
29, 37, 44-66, 81-82, 88,
90-95, 97-99

Limited Partnerships · 39,
   41-43

M

Medicare tax · 19-20, 70,
   84, 99

O

Operating Agreements ·
   47, 53

P

Partnership Agreements ·
   27-29, 31, 47
Pass-Through Entities ·
   17, 21, 30, 37, 45, 55,
   71, 83, 86
Personal Service
   Corporations · 65-66,
   72-74
Piercing the Corporate Veil
   · 77, 79, 100

R

Reasonable Salary · 84-86,
   99

Registered Limited
   Liability Partnership ·
   52

S

Schedule K · 31-32, 34
Schedule K-1 · 31-32, 34
S-Corporations · 7, 9, 37,
   44, 56, 64, 66, 76, 80-86,
   90, 94, 96-97, 99-100
Self-Employment Tax ·
   19-21, 33-34, 69, 84-86,
   99
Sole Proprietorships · 8-9,
   11-17, 19-22, 24-27, 29-
   31, 34, 39, 48, 53-55, 57,
   59, 67, 69, 72, 74, 83,
   92-100
State Taxes · 57-59

T

Tax Brackets · 18-19, 32,
   68, 70

U

Unlimited Liability · 22-24,
   39, 41, 43, 55, 60

LaVergne, TN USA
04 June 2010
185046LV00001B/128/P

9 780981 454207